Leadership Styles

| Directing | Discussing | Delegating |

◄──────── Diagnose What's Needed ────────►

Are you achieving the desired results?

Paul B. Thornton

Copyright © 2022 by Paul B. Thornton
All rights reserved.

ISBN | x-xxx-xxxxx-x

Dedication
To Dr. Paul Hersey

He was my favorite professor at Ohio University. His course, "Managing Organizational Behavior" was outstanding. He taught me the Situational Leadership Model (developed by him and Dr. Ken Blanchard) and demonstrated how to apply it by the way he taught his course.

Professor Hersey inspired me to be a life-long student and teacher of leadership.

Introduction

Welcome!

Various articles and books have described numerous leadership styles including:

- Assertive
- Autocratic
- Change Agent
- Coaching
- Country Club
- Collaborative
- Delegating
- Laissez-faire
- Participatory
- Servant
- Visionary

Are there really that many different styles? No.

I believe there are three basic styles that parents, teachers, coaches, managers, project leaders, presidents, and team leaders use every day.

- ➢ Directing
- ➢ Discussing
- ➢ Delegating

When you use the appropriate leadership style (directing, discussing or delegating), you help people achieve the desired goals. In addition, you help upgrade people's skills and develop character traits that are imperative to their success.

It sounds easy—*just use the appropriate style and everything works out*. Like a lot of things in life, the ideas aren't complicated, but executing them is challenging. It takes a lot of practice and learning to consistently get it right.

What are some of the challenges related to each style?

1. Directing Style—Some people are too direct; others sugarcoat their message or talk in vague, general terms. Some people talk down to people and others micromanage.
2. Discussing Style—Some people do too much talking and not enough listening. Some people only want to tell people what to do. Others engage in analysis paralysis and never make decisions.
3. Delegating Style—Some people can't let go; they want to be involved in every decision. Others over delegate to their star performers and under delegate to everyone else.

Most people have a default leadership style, that they like to use. But it doesn't always align with what the person or situation needs at the moment.

I am on a mission to help you use the leadership style that best aligns with what the situation requires.

Chapters 3 through 9 provide information about using each leadership style when communicating, establishing goals, coaching, solving problems, influencing others, and holding people accountable.

My Research

For the past 35 years, I have observed, studied, and interviewed leaders about the approach and style they use in various situations. We have discussed what works best and why. And what's ineffective and why.

For this book, I interviewed a variety of people including CEOs, athletic coaches, college professors, firefighter, grandparent, minister, parents, presidents, managers, salesmen, teachers, vice presidents, and team leaders. They all use each of the three styles in their day-today activities. Their comments appear at the end of each chapter.

Thank You

For buying my book.

Please share your thoughts about the 3Ds and post a short review on AMAZON.

Table of Contents

Chapter 1   The Three Leadership Styles 1

Chapter 2   Which Leadership Style Should You Use xx

Chapter 3   Communicating xx

Chapter 4   Setting Goals xx

Chapter 5   Coaching xx

Chapter 6   Influencing People xx

Chapter 7   Solving Problems and Making Decisions xx

Chapter 8   Resolving Conflicts xx

Chapter 9   Holding People Accountable xx

Chapter 10   Providing the Right Amount xx

Chapter 11   Continuous Improvement xx

About the Author xx

Recommended Books and Articles xx

Chapter 1
The Three Leadership Styles

Each style—directing, discussing, and delegating—is unique in terms of how you interact with people.

The Directing Style—You tell the person or group the following:

- What to do
- How to do it
- When to have it completed by

Using the directing style, you assign roles and responsibilities, set standards, and define expectations.

The directing style is appropriate when people lack experience and don't know what to do. My first summer job was painting boats. I was clueless on what to do. I needed direction. I needed my supervisor to tell me exactly what to do.

This style is also appropriate in emergency situations when there is no time for discussion, collaboration, or brainstorming.

The directing style promotes learning through observing the speaker, listening, and following directions.

When using the directing style, you should recognize and reward people for doing exactly what you told them to do.

In recent years, there has been strong criticism of the "Command and Control" (or directing) approach to managing and leading. Some authors and experts make it sound like it's the worst thing you could ever do. I disagree. In certain situations, commanding or directing is needed and very appropriate. When people lack knowledge and skills, they need direction. It is essential for newbies to be told what to do and how to do things at first.

However, when command and control or directing is used in the wrong situations or turns into micromanagement, it is very ineffective and demotivating.

The Discussing Style—Over 2,000 years ago, Socrates realized that leading was more a matter of asking the right questions than giving all the answers.

Using the discussing style, you ask questions to solicit people's ideas on the problems and opportunities that you are addressing. Discussions are used to clarify problems, identify opportunities, and evaluate options to pursue.

As people grow and develop, they need to see the bigger picture. Asking questions that broaden people's thinking is helpful.

In some discussions, you are an equal member of the group (diagram on the left) sharing your ideas as well as listening and responding to the ideas of others. In other situations, you are in the middle of the group leading the discussion and acting as a facilitator.

The discussing style promotes learning by requiring people to think and express their ideas clearly and succinctly. People also

Discussing Style

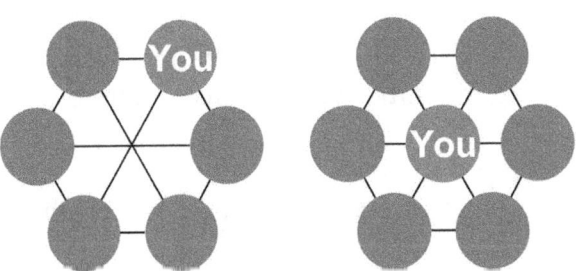

learn the importance of supporting their ideas with examples, evidence, and data.

The discussing approach is appropriate when people have some experience and confidence in speaking up. This style is also effective to capture "lessons learned" after a project has been completed.

When using the discussing style, praise people for contributing to the discussion and building on the ideas of others.

After a healthy discussion, you alone may make the decision on how to proceed, or the group may reach a consensus that everyone supports.

Delegating Style—Delegation involves describing a project or task to someone and explaining the desired goal and deadline. How they get the work done is left up to them.

The person or team is empowered to take action and do what's needed.

The delegating style promotes learning by doing. People learn as they deal with problems, evaluate options, influence others, and make decisions.

The delegating style is appropriate when people have the experience and skills to do what's needed to get the task completed on time and within budget.

When using the delegating style, reward people for working independently, taking the initiative, meeting deadlines, and producing quality work.

As people gain experience, you have to loosen the reins. Allow them to do more on their own.

Results Achieved

Results can be viewed in two ways:

1. Task Results—The task or project gets completed on schedule. The finished product meets or exceeds the required expectations.
2. People Results—The person or team develops their competencies and character traits such as confidence, honesty, and being responsible.

Over the past 10 years, I have seen several versions of this statement by Tom Peters, *Great leaders don't create followers, they create more leaders*. How do they do it? As you move from a directing style to a discussing style to a delegating style, you are helping people develop the skills, maturity, and independence to be a leader. You help people learn to think, present their ideas, and take decisive action.

If you correctly use all three styles, you will develop more leaders. However, if you only use the directing style, you create more followers. People who wait to told what to do.

Your goals should be to develop your children, students, employees, and team members so they are more capable and confident to handle all the challenges they face.

Comments from Practitioners

John P. Murphy—Scituate Fire Department, Chief of Department and Emergency Management Director

"**Directing Style**—In all emergency situations, I use a directing style. There is no time for discussion and collaboration. Decisions must be made quickly. In non-emergency situations, I use a directing style when specific tasks need to be accomplished by a specific date. Putting directions in writing—sending emails is helpful. Establishing deadlines is critical.

Discussing Style—I think it is very important to utilize the strengths of all my employees. I discuss problems and issues with the people who have the appropriate expertise. My approach is—seek out the experts and get their input before making any decisions. In some cases, it's educational for me to probe their ideas and recommendations to understand their thinking. One way I keep learning is through collaboration and discussion.

Delegating Style—People have different goals and interests. I try to delegate projects that align with people's interests. People are more motivated to excel in areas that interest them. When I delegate a project, I want the person to take ownership and be responsible for doing great work and meeting all deadlines. When delegation goes wrong—the task wasn't done as expected, it's important to get the facts before jumping to any conclusions. Ask the person for their view of what happened."

Beth McGinnis-Cavanaugh—Professor, Engineering and Physical Sciences at Springfield Technical Community College

"I use the three Ds to create meaningful learning experiences. At the course level, **directing** entails offering students clear goals, clear expectations, and clear pathways to success.

Open and authentic **discussions** allow me to connect with students and ask questions that force them to challenge their beliefs and think independently and creatively. Through discussion, I try to establish a safe, collaborative, and welcoming course spaces that promote strong relationships and interactions.

Delegating requires students to take charge of their learning and performance. This approach teaches students how to advocate for themselves, to ask for help, to communicate, to seek needed resources, and to work independently."

Chapter 2
Which Leadership Style Should You Use?

It depends.

It depends on the person—his skills and experience relative to the task or challenge that he faces.

Each person has a unique set of strengths and experiences. They are strong in some areas and need help in others.

Doctors make diagnostic judgements before prescribing various medications and treatments. When symptoms and conditions change, doctors change their recommendations.

The best leaders use a similar approach. They diagnose people's skillset and mindset relative to the challenges they face. They then decide what actions to take to help them.

When diagnosing the current situation, focus on both the task and the people.

The Task

Answering these questions can help you understand the task or challenge that people face.

1. Is the task or problem clearly defined? If the task isn't clearly defined what information is needed to define it more precisely?
2. Has the task been done before?
3. Have requirements changed?
4. What resources does the task or project require?
5. What are the time constraints?
6. What types of decisions will the task require?
7. How does the task fit into the bigger strategic picture?

The People

Consider people's ability, motivation, and experience to do the required work?

- **Ability**—Does the person or team have the knowledge, skills, confidence, and time to do what is needed?
- **Motivation**—Is the person or team motivated to do what's required?
- **Experience**—Has the person or team done the task before? Were they successful?

Once your diagnosis is done, decide which leadership style will be most helpful. The most appropriate style provides the right amount of direction, discussion, and empowerment to help people succeed.

As people gain more experience, you need to alter your style. Generally, you move from a directing style to a discussing style to a delegating style.

What happens if you only use one style?

If you only use a directing style, what happens? People wait to be told what to do and then respond. They never learn to think for themselves or make decisions on their own. Their self-confidence is limited. They become overly dependent on the leader, parent, teacher, or coach.

- If you only use a discussing style, what happens? The building burns down while you are having a meeting. Analysis paralysis becomes common. People never learn to make timely decisions or learn how to implement their decisions.
- If you only use a delegating style, what happens? People get confused and feel overwhelmed. In many cases, they don't know what to do which results in poor quality and late deliveries. Their performance is ineffective and inefficient.

Don't be a one-style leader. Increase your effectiveness by using the leadership style that fits the needs of the situation.

Unusual and Complex Situations

Most of the time, it is fairly easy and straightforward to determine which style to use. However, it some situations it's more challenging.

When faced with unusual and complex situations, it's helpful to pause and consider these factors:

- What new issues, challenges, or requirements are impacting the task or the people?
- What's unknown about the current project? What facts are in dispute?
- Are additional resources required?
- Have new priorities surfaced that will impact this project?

The answers to these questions will help you determine which style would be most effective. In some cases, it's best to start with a discussing style and then decide which direction to go in. Do people need more direction or more empowerment?

Summary

Effective diagnosis requires you to analyze both the people and the task they face.

Proper diagnosis helps you determine what people need to perform at their best.

When you use the right style, you do two things. You help people:

1. Get the task done.
2. Develop the skills and character traits needed for continued success.

Comments from Practitioners

John P. Murphy—Scituate Fire Department, Chief of Department and Emergency Management Director

"Each style is useful in certain situations. Some things I consider before deciding which style to use include: the urgency of the task, the expertise of the person, the history of previous interactions with the person, and what would help the person grow and develop."

Mary Jean Thornton—former Executive Vice President and College Professor

"If the person has little or no experience and limited skills, I use a directing style.

If the person has some skills and experience related to the task, I use a discussing style. I ask questions to determine what actions they will take to complete the task.

If the person has significant experience, I delegate. I let him do it his way. I continue to monitor the individual, in the event there is a need to assist."

When conditions change, I alter my approach. I usually take a gradual change from one style to another."

--------Diagnose the Situation--------

Chapter 3
Communicating

Your ideas need a proper balance between having optimism for improvement and realism about the obstacles that must be overcome.

Communication takes place in both one-on-one interactions and in group settings. The ability to send clear messages, ask the right questions, and listen carefully is vital.

Your messages need to direct, engage, and empower people to do what's required.

What you say and how you say it are both very important.

Each style—directing, discussing, delegating—requires a different approach when communicating.

Approaches to Communicating

- **Directing Style**—You tell people what to do and how to do it. You do most of the talking and hopefully they do a lot of listening.

  Make sure you have the person's undivided attention. Making eye contact helps.

  Be direct and to the point. Do not use 50 words to say something you could say with 10 words. Scrap what's unnecessary.

When giving directions, start with the big picture and then go into the details. Other points to remember:

1. If possible, show the person the desired output. Give them a concrete example of what you want.
2. Provide written instructions if your directions are complex or lengthy.
3. Avoid using jargon and acronyms the person may not understand.

Don't overcomplicate your message with excessive details. Provide the most relevant information, so they know exactly what to do.

No matter how great a communicator you are, understanding will never be automatic. Check to make sure your directions are understood.

Test the transfer. Ask the person to explain in his or her own words what you want done.

- **Discussing Style**—You ask questions that focus on what needs to be done and how it should be done. You solicit people's ideas and recommendations.

Communication is two-way.

Great discussions require great questions. So, prepare questions in advance.

Don't lead the witness. Ask questions that let the person express their ideas, not what you want to hear.

Ask one question at a time and listen carefully to their answer.

Observe body language. What non-verbal messages are being sent?

Leadership Styles

In group settings, don't allow one or two people to dominate the discussion. Get everyone involved. Don't allow the introverts to remain silent. Withhold your opinion until others have had a chance to comment.

The amount of discussion required on a topic is influenced by several factors such as priority, complexity, time constraints, and the number of people involved.

Avoid unproductive discussions. We have all experienced those meetings where the person with the big ego rambles on and on. Little progress is made.

On the other hand, don't cut the discussion off too quickly. When that happens, people feel disappointed and less committed to the plans and decisions made.

The right amount of discussion starts by identifying the critical questions that need to be addressed and ends when everyone has had a chance to state their opinion.

- **Delegating Style**—You are empowering the person or team to work on their own and get the task done.

It's important you communicate confidence in the person's abilities and motivation to do what's needed. *I'm confident you are going to do a great job on this project.*

Remember what legendary NFL coach Bill Walsh once said, "The four most powerful words are: I believe in you."

Once you delegate a task, refrain from giving advice. Let the person figure out what to do. Certainly, it may be appropriate for you to answer some questions, but let them make decisions on their own. That affirms your confidence in their abilities.

People who have the "rescuer personality" have great difficulty here. They keep jumping back in to help the person. Too much helping negatively impacts the person's opportunity to learn what it means to be responsible and take initiative.

Summary—Communications

As a parent, teacher, coach, manager, and team leader, consider the following:

1. *Directing Style*—Directions that are clear, concise, and complete prevent communication breakdowns. Praise people for following directions.
2. *Discussing Style*—The better your question; the better the discussion. Recognize people for contributing, collaborating, and building on the ideas of others.
3. *Delegating Style*—Affirm people and trust that they will get the job done. Reward people for being responsible, taking initiative, and working independently.

Effective communication skills—both speaking and listening are required when using each of the leadership styles.

Comments from Practitioners

Mary Jean Thornton, Grandparent

"I have five grandsons who teach me new lessons about communications all the time. Making eye contact, asking questions, listening, and not allowing—'I don't know'—answers are a few of the topics we frequently discuss.

Directing style—I have no trouble being direct. But if you are too direct, you are viewed as intimidating and harsh. That is not good. People do not speak up in that type of environment. I want my grandsons to be direct and honest with me. On occasion, I have to say to them, *'Don't hold back, tell me what you think.'*

Discussing style—The right question invites people into the conversation. But I've learned that I have to be patient and aware as to when my grandsons want to discuss various topics. Just because I want to discuss ABC, doesn't mean they do. Timing is important.

Delegating style—Communicating what I want done is easy as long as I have their undivided attention. Holding them accountable for results is very important. *'You said you were going to text me after each game and...'* Our words and actions send important messages."

C V Nagarajan, CEO—Dutco Tennant LLC

"I use all three styles. Emphasis has been more on the delegating style because it suits our culture in the UAE.

Directing style—It is important to be clear and precise giving people the required information to avoid any misunderstanding. Directing people in a straightforward, focused manner yet treating them with respect has been helpful.

Discussing style—This style is useful when my colleagues identify challenges or ideas for implementation that they want to discuss. I use questions to unearth the details, assumptions, and people's feelings etc. I often ask, 'What have you tried so far and what happened?' I find this is a useful question to ask and then listen intently and enthusiastically. This question not only offers a chance for introspection by the employee, but also leads to a productive discussion of other options to consider.

Delegating style—This style is used most often in our workplace. To communicate empowerment, you need to treat people like owners. You need to remind people that they are responsible for results. Employees adapt to the changing ground situation and modify their actions to achieve the desired outcome. People display entrepreneurial skills and become creative when they are empowered. This style also enhances employee happiness and produces more engagement."

Chapter 4
Establishing Goals and Plans

Goals indicate what's important. They need to support the organization's overall strategic plan.

Goals need to be relevant, meaningful, and achievable for the people involved.

Goals with deadlines motivate people to set priorities and schedule their work.

When conditions change, goals and plans need to be reviewed and updated.

Each leadership style—directing, discussing, delegating—uses a different approach to establishing goals and plans.

Approaches to Establishing Goals and Plans

- **Directing Style**—In some cases, you know exactly what you want done and how you want it done. In other situations, customers and people higher up the ladder have already defined the goal and plan. You are simply passing along the directions.

    Be precise in stating what you want done. Vague goals such as "improve quality" or "cut your expenses" are open to interpretation and can create confusion.

    Always establish a deadline to have the work completed.

    Once you have the goal nailed down, explain the plan—how the goal will be achieved. Describe the actions you want the person to take.

Test for understanding. Ask them to explain the goal and the actions they will be taking.

Explain what's in it for them. Increase people's motivation by explaining why the goal is important to them and what they will learn in the process.

- **Discussing Style**—When there are opportunities to influence the goal and plan, a discussing style may be appropriate. Getting people's ideas and input increases their ownership and motivation. It also may lead to a better goal and plan.

People want to be involved and have a say in establishing goals and creating plans that directly impact them.

Start with the goal. Explaining the context or big picture. Then, solicit people's input on what the goal should be and why. Probe their reasoning. *Why do you think the goal should be a 13% increase in sales?*

Test to find out if everyone believes the goal is achievable.

After you get agreement on the goal, discuss the plan.

To create a plan, ask questions like these.

- ✓ What are all the actions required to achieve the goal?
- ✓ What timeframes are needed for each step in the plan?
- ✓ What people and resources are needed to do each step of the plan?
- ✓ Who should be assigned which tasks?

As people mature and grow, let them discuss the plan by themselves. You can be an observer and comment only if necessary.

Put the goal and plan in writing. Distribute it to all the people who have a need to know.

- **Delegating Style**—When people know what to do or can figure it out, they don't need direction. They don't need to have a discussion. They need to be empowered.

However, it may be necessary to have a follow-up meeting to review their goals and plans. Also, if it's a major project, establish periodic dates to review their progress.

You could also delegate the task of having a team member prepare and deliver a presentation on the steps required to establish and implement an effective plan. This information could help everyone in your group learn more about effective planning.

Summary—Goals and Plans

As a parent, teacher, coach, manager, and team leader, consider the following:

1. *Directing Style*—Some goals and plans aren't negotiable. Tell people what must be done and why it's important.
2. *Discussing Style*—Soliciting people input increases their ownership and motivation.
3. *Delegating Style*—Empower people to come up with their own goals and plans and review them with you. What they come up with may surprise you.

Conditions can change quickly. Goals and plans may need to be updated on a regular basis.

Comments from Practitioners

Gail Olmsted, Parent, College Professor, and former Manager

"I used all three styles every day.

When it comes to goal setting, **directing** helped me specify exactly what I wanted done. I was able to set precise goals and also indicate how I wanted the task completed. When directing people, I learned it's important to confirm that the directions I provided were clear and well understood. Asking questions to determine understanding is an important step in the process.

Discussing requires more time and patience, but will lead to improved performance in the long run. *What is your goal for extracurricular activities this year? What is your goal for today's meeting with our new customer?* When I involved people in setting goals, I found it's important to ensure that everyone has an opportunity to contribute ideas and that the final plan or strategy is agreed to and supported by all.

Delegating requires confidence and trust. It tells others—I believe that you have the ability to figure out how to get this household chore or assignment or project at work completed. When I let people establish their own goals, I found they were more motivated as they were able to build on their skills and past experiences. It is important to build in opportunities to connect at key points during the process in order to ensure that everything is on track."

Dr. Nido R. Qubein, President, High Point University

"My primary goal as a leader is to create capacity in others. To ensure that our vision and our reality match.

Directing is a style I employ to give concise and clear guidelines on how to achieve our goals and objectives. In my group sessions, I ask questions like "Who are we now? Who do we want to become? How do we get there?" and I give recommendations on how we can answer these questions purposefully. Our passion and our purpose must be in sync, and clear directions pave the way. I have learned that a team will follow a leader who has crystal clarity about mission, vision, and values of the organization and can teach them.

Discussing is an on-going team process where we debate and dissect ideas and challenges – both on transactional and transformational levels – in order to "connect" not just "communicate" with each other and do it with persuasion. We may discuss matters such as the viability of our business, its volatility, and its vitality. We discuss ways to improve our skill of judgment, our desire to enhance awareness, and to guarantee relevance at all levels. I learn so much about my colleagues when we discuss openly, fairly, and respectfully.

Delegating is a necessary skill for every leader if we are to multiply ourselves and accomplish more. It is also a helpful tool to 'inspect what we expect' through observation and measurement. A leader can be a better coach when he or she can delegate a task or a project and explain the result of what we do. Why it works. Why it does not. I have learned that sometimes it is frustrating and time-consuming to delegate when I can deal with the matter myself … but the only way to grow a team is to educate them through experiential learning."

Chapter 5
Coaching

Every coach, parent, teacher, supervisor, manager, project leader, and team leader know the importance of effective coaching.

Coaching works when the student is open and receptive (so timing is important).

Coaching works when the teacher is clear and precise.

Before you start coaching, make multiple observations of the person's performance. Look for patterns. What do they do well? What could they do better?

Performance gaps may be caused by any of these factors.

- The person lacks ability or motivation
- The person doesn't understand certain aspects of the job
- There are internal or external obstacles interfering with the person's ability to perform

Coaching involves helping people add and subtract. What do I mean?

Sometimes you have to help the person add new perspectives and skills to their toolbox. For example, you may have to help a person learn a new skill to better manage his time.

On the other hand, you may have to help a person subtract or eliminate something they are doing that doesn't add value such as focusing on low priority items and procrastinating.

Approaches to Coaching

- **Directing Style**—Sometimes it's effective to simply tell the person what they need to stop doing or start doing. I have a tennis coach who does just that. He not only tells me what to do, but also demonstrates the proper technique.

  In some cases, it is best to describe the person's current behavior and the results it is producing. People must recognize there is a problem before they are motivated to change.

  Effective coaches break down complex tasks in to bite size pieces. Then explain how to do each part and how all the pieces fit together.

- **Discussing Style**—Sometimes the best coaching is done through discussion. Getting people's input helps you understand what they're thinking.

  Ask questions to discuss what he did and why he did it. *What was your goal? Why did you do XYZ? What do you think you did well? What could be improved?*

  Ask questions to uncover the specific changes that are required to improve. *What do you need to do to run a more effective meeting?*

  Every coach knows that improving your performance requires a lot of practice and feedback to get it right. Determine the person's commitment to doing what's needed. *Are you committed to making the required changes? Are you committed to following this plan?*

- **Delegating Style**—In essence, you are asking the person to do some self-coaching. Part of people's development is gaining the ability to critique their own performance and self-correct as needed. Some athletes are able to improve their performance as the game goes on.

David Novak, former CEO of YUM Brands said that he had self-coached himself throughout his career. Take time to know yourself. Learn from your successes and setbacks. When Novak didn't reach a goal, he changed his thinking from "not accomplished" to "not *yet* accomplished."

When coaching an employee, you might say something like the following:

> *I want you to think about your performance on this assignment. Identify three things you did well and one area that needs improvement. I'd like to meet tomorrow at 2:00 P. M. to hear what you come up with.*

Here are additional examples of using the delegating style to coach.

If the person needs to improve his presentation skills, have him observe and interview three top presenters. Ask the person to determine the guiding principles each of the top presenters use in preparing and delivering their presentations.

Assume you are coaching the person on improving her time management skills. Delegate the task of having her do a short seminar at your next staff meeting on "The Principles of Effective Time Management." Have the student become the teacher.

Summary—Coaching

As a parent, teacher, coach, manager, and team leader, consider the following:

1. *Directing Style*—Tell them what to do or demonstrate how to do it. Remind people that building competence requires practice, feedback, and reflection.
2. *Discussing Style*—Ask questions that require people to think about what they are doing and what changes would be beneficial.
3. *Delegating Style*—Empower people to critique their own performance so they become proficient at self-coaching.

If the person is defensive and not-open to feedback, you have to address that issue first. Coaching sessions always require follow-up.

Comments from Practitioners

Bob Emery, former Head Hockey Coach, Plattsburg State University

"I coach hockey, but I'm really teaching leadership, life skills, and teamwork. In the old days I used a lot of **directing** when coaching. 'Do this. Do not do that.' Today I do a lot more **discussing** and **delegating.** I ask a lot of questions to see what the player is thinking. I delegate when I want the players to do self-reflection and self-analysis. For example, players must critique their play after each game by watching videotapes. Each player discusses his self-analysis with one of the coaches to make sure we are all on the same page. Coaching is productive when real learning occurs. This happens best when the player is engaged and takes ownership for his performance both on and off the ice."

Michael Lambert, Team Leader, Materials Science Lab, Kamatics Corporation

"To determine how much or how little coaching is needed, I take steps to understand the challenges my employees face in doing their day-to-day work. In addition, I make it a priority to learn their strengths and weaknesses, how they perform under pressure, and what motivates them.

I tailor my coaching to each individual. Some people need constant coaching and guidance, while others are independent, eager to learn, and task driven. Everyone is different.

I've learned it's important to stay flexible. As people grow and change for better or worse, the amount and type of coaching needed also changes. Focusing on the quality and timeliness of coaching, rather than how much or how little coaching to provide, has proven helpful in finding the right balance."

Chapter 6
Influencing People

Parents, grandparents, teachers, coaches, ministers, managers, and team leaders know that there are times when you need to influence people to accept your ideas, standards, and proposals.

Three of the most common ways you influence people include:

- Setting a positive example
- Encouraging others
- Having passion when delivering your message

You can also influence people by appealing to their head, heart, and hands.

What do I mean?

- **The Head**—Appeal to their intellect. Present the hard-hitting facts and indisputable logic. Persuade people through rational arguments, including market research, customer surveys, and case studies.
- **The Heart**—Appeal to their emotions. *Pull at their heartstrings!* People are motivated by things that make them feel better. Connect to people's needs for status, order, honor, security, and purpose.
- **The Hands**—Persuade people through a direct experience. Action statements like *"Take the car for a test drive,"* or *"Do a taste test"* give people something to experience viscerally. Sometimes the best way to sell a product or service is to have people try it.

Blaise Pascal (French mathematician and master of prose) once said, "People are usually more convinced by reasons they discover themselves than those found out by others." So, after you make your case, ask questions such as:

- What do these facts mean to you?
- How do you feel about…?
- What impact did this experience have on you?

Whatever approach you use to influence people, you must answer the question: "What's in it for them?" How will they benefit?

People support ideas that satisfy their needs and create positive feelings.

The final step in influencing people is asking for the sale. Every sales rep knows the importance of this cardinal rule. Close the deal by asking for people commitment.

- ❖ *Will you support my proposal in today's meeting?*
- ❖ *Will you try my suggestion for the next 30 days?*

Approaches to Influencing People

- **Directing Style**

    Tell people how your idea will improve their situation. Sell the benefits. Emphasize what's in it for them.

    Present the compelling evidence and facts that support your proposal.

    Create a sense of urgency to increase people's motivation. *If we don't take action in the next 7-days, we lose the opportunity.*

Deliver your message with confidence and conviction. When you demonstrate a strong point of view, others take notice.

- **Discussing Style**
  Ask questions that will do one or more of the following:

  - Create interest and curiosity in your ideas
  - Frame a problem in a way that creates new opportunities
  - Identify gaps between "what is" and "what could be"
  - Identify beliefs or assumptions that may no longer be accurate

  The right questions can motivate people to want to learn more about your ideas.

  Listen carefully to what's said. Notice what isn't said. Ask follow-up questions to discuss the concerns people have about your ideas.

  When you're dealing with closed-minded people, start by asking questions that begin to move them from "no interest" to "some curiosity." Provide additional information and ask them to review it for discussion at your next meeting.

  It's can be a slow process. It may take multiple discussions before the person is willing to consider your proposal.

- **Delegating Style**
  Using this style, you influence people through a direct experience. For example, when the salesperson says *"Try this product for the next 30 days"* they are trying to influence you by providing a direct experience.

In a similar way, you can influence people by having them:

- ➤ Interview upset customers
- ➤ Observe a top performing team
- ➤ Go shopping at the local grocery store and focus on how you are treated when you ask for help

Direct experience provides insights and feelings you won't get from an email or reading a report.

Summary—Influencing

As a parent, teacher, coach, manager, and team leader, consider the following:

1. *Directing Style*—Describe all the benefits that will occur when your idea is implemented. Include what's in it for them.
2. *Discussing Style*—Ask people to think about how they will feel when your idea or proposal is implemented. Feelings and emotions can motivate people to support your new initiatives.
3. *Delegating Style*—Provide the right experience to impact the way people feel about your proposal.

Using words and stories that connect to people's head and heart can move them to take action. Also, get help and support from your allies.

Comments from Practitioners

Fred Kelly, VP Sales Medical Device Company

"The ability to influence people with Positive Intent is an important skill everyone needs including parents, coaches, teachers, managers, and sales reps.

For me, influencing people starts with doing research before meeting with them. I try to discover as much as I can about the customer's current situation—their goals and problems. Research includes talking with employees, competitors, vendors as well as doing online research.

You build tremendous credibility by doing your homework prior to a meeting. Preparation leads to productive results. It also avoids potential pitfalls like discovering a problem that you cannot resolve.

After completing the research, I prepare questions. The right questions are vital to building rapport and trust as well as gaining a deeper understanding of the customer's problems. The more focused the questions are about their current situation, the more value there is in the customer's response.

Mr. Customer from my research and conversations with your team, they mentioned your green widget wasn't working for you. How is the green widget impacting your business negatively?

Once a problem is discovered/defined, it's important to have the person acknowledge this issue and agree they want to solve it.

Mr. customer you stated that the green widget is causing a decrease in your production. If my solution could correct that issue, would you like to understand how?

Regarding the 3Ds

Directing—Once the problem has been mutually agreed upon, I tell the person or group how my product will solve their problem. I back it up with data, from other customers and trusted sources (Customer Testimonials, White papers, Consumer Reports, etc.).

Discussing—Some of my guiding principles include: prepare questions in advance. Prepare questions that focus on both defining the problem and identifying the implications to the business. Listen more than I talk, take copious notes, and be aware of what isn't stated.

Delegating—Having customers view a live demonstration to see the positive benefits of your product or idea is a powerful way to influence them."

Andy Thornton, Sales Rep for National Lumber

"I sell building supplies such as lumber, windows, roofing materials, siding, and new kitchens to home builders and general contractors.

Directing Style—I try to influence customers by telling them the positive attributes of my company. Some of the things I often mention include: how long the company has been in business, family owned, debt free, owning two truss plants, and having our own kitchen design teams.

I also tell home builders, remodelers, and general contractors what they can expect from me. Early morning and weekend deliveries, when necessary, quick turnaround on getting back to them, up-to-date product knowledge and in general, great service.

Telling people how great you are must be followed up with great performance. Having said that, I try to be very honest and candid with all customers. I tell them the good stuff but also admit when I have made mistakes and what I did to correct them.

Finally, I tell customers all the features and benefits of the new products we introduce.

Discussing Style—The right question can influence customers. I try to ask thoughtful questions that are relevant to their business needs. Some of my favorite questions include:

- What is the one area you'd like to see improvement with your current supplier?
- Is price as important as service?
- What do you like and dislike about your current suppliers?
- What can I do to help you succeed?
- What additional product options would you like to be able to offer your homeowners?

The right question can open people's mind to consider new ideas and options.

Delegating Style—On occasion I have given a product to a builder or general contractor and asked them to try it and see what they think. But, most of the delegating I do is to Kevin, my inside sales rep. He is very talented and motivated, so he readily accepts the tasks I ask him to do. A few things I have learned about delegating is that it requires trust and builds trust. It also gives me a good understanding of who is good at what.

Each customer is unique and they face many challenges in running their business. In all sales situations, I try to think about the best approach I can use to build relationships, sell products, and help them succeed."

Chapter 7
Solving Problems and Making Decisions

No matter what role you are performing—parent, teacher, coach, project leader—dealing with problems is included in the job description.

Problems come in all shapes and sizes. Some are routine and easy to solve. Others are big and require significant research and analysis.

Three important questions to consider when confronted with a problem:

- Who owns the problem? (Just because you're presented with a problem doesn't necessarily mean it's yours to solve.)
- How much time, effort, and money should go into solving the problem? (Not all problems are equal in importance.)
- What approach should you use to address the problem? (Get personally involved, delegate it to someone else etc.)

The common steps found in most problem solving/decision-making models include:

1. Define the problem
2. Identify possible solutions
3. Evaluate options
4. Make a decision

Approaches to Solving Problems and Making Decisions

- **Directing Style**—You define the problem and make all decisions. You tell people what they need to do.

  In some situations, it may be appropriate to explain why you are making a particular decision to help people understand your thinking. It teaches others what to consider when making decisions.

  Competent leaders also know that some issue like terminating a direct report should never be delegated. They own it and must make the final decisions.

- **Discussing Style**—You ask questions to solicit people's ideas regarding each step in the problem solving/decision-making process.

  - *How would you define the problem? (Separate symptoms from the underlying problem, ask 'why" multiple times)*
  - *What do you think are possible options to solve it?*
  - *What are the advantages and disadvantages of each option?*
  - *What decision would you make? Why that decision?*

  In group settings, if there is too much agreement, it may indicate "groupthink." Everyone is simply going along with the group to maintain harmony. If you sense groupthink is occurring, play the devil's advocate and encourage opposing viewpoints.

  After hearing everyone's comments, you may make the final decision or the group may reach consensus on how to proceed.

- **Delegating Style**—You assign the problem to one or more people and require them to solve it. Establish a deadline to have the problem solved.

When delegating long-term projects, establish periodic review dates to access progress.

Beware of reverse delegation. Sounds strange, but it happens. It occurs when a person tries to give back a task that you assigned to them. Always keep ownership of solving the problem with them.

Summary—Problem Solving and Decision Making

As a parent, teacher, coach, manager, and team leader, consider the following:

1. *Directing Style*—Some problems and solutions are simple and straightforward. Just tell people what to do.
2. *Discussing Style*—Some problems are vague and unclear. Have a discussion with the right people to define the problem and identify possible solutions.
3. *Delegating Style*—Empower people to solve problems on their own. This builds their skills and confidence.

You seldom have perfect information, but they still have to make timely decisions. Trust your intuition when you have had significant experience in the problem area.

Comments from Practitioners

Kate Thornton Labor, Parent and Senior Vice President

"**Directing** – During recess, my youngest son, Keegan (age7) was having some issues with Johnny on the infamous school playground. I directed him to do three things:

1. Tell a teacher if Johnny started anything with him
2. Distance himself from Johnny on the playground

3. Do not talk about Johnny's behavior or not liking him to any of his other friends

I repeated this daily until Keegan stopped talking about a daily incident on the playground. Problem solved.

Lesson Learned: There are times when you need to direct your child to get to the desired behavior and you may need to direct him multiple times.

Discussing – I have found if my child is part of the discussion, he feels more connected to the desired outcome and more willing to do the required work. Let us take my middle son, Noah, (age 10). Prior to this school year, he did not like reading – actually, he did not really see a need for it. So, we talked about why he did not like reading. It turns out, he did not like the books I was selecting. He shared what he was interested in reading. He also wanted his own library card to select his own books. When he did the book selecting, he became a highly-motivated reader. Problem solved.

Lesson Learned: There are times when it is best to let your child be part of the decision-making process. You also find out what they are interested in versus just assuming you know what they like.

Delegating – I have learned teenagers like my son Owen (age 14), often don't like being directed and aren't always thrilled about having a discussion. So delegating is often the best option. Like most teenagers, Owen has a phone and let us just say, it could be an extension of his body – he's on it often. His agreed monthly fee for his phone is $45. However, one month the charge jumped up to $150. I could have directed him to change his behavior or discuss the increase. But I didn't. I delegated the task to him. I asked him to figure out why the monthly charge was so high and then give me his plan for how he was going to get it back down to the expected

$45/month. And, he did. Turned out, he was streaming music – like lots of music versus downloading and creating a playlist.

Lesson Learned: When you delegate, you extend ownership which gives your child a sense of feeling independent. They get tasks completed when the task is *important* to them."

Julie Erickson, Executive and Leadership Coach

"I've found that asking someone what they think is causing the behavior is a good start to coming up with a solution, together. When they say 'I don't know,' I ask, 'Well, what if you did know? What do you think might be the reason?' Usually, they have an answer then. The conversation can then begin.

I can speak to solving long-standing lateness issues with colleagues and team members. I start by saying, 'I've noticed that you are usually late." Avoid the 'always' word which is often a trigger for defensiveness. 'Is that something you've noticed as well?' is a good follow-up question to see if the other person is aware and will own the problem. That's probably 80% of the issue. Once someone owns the problem, they usually want to solve it and welcome help."

Chapter 8
Resolving Conflicts

In every relationship—husband-wife, manager-employee, leader-follower, parent-child, teacher-student, coach athlete, friend-friend—there are conflicts.

Conflicts involve people. People have feelings and they influence how conflicts are discussed and resolved.

Conflicts can lead to productive discussions that produce creative solutions and improved relationships. Or, conflicts can be heated, emotional, and lead to personal attacks. People get defensive and stop listening.

Having emotional intelligence and being empathetic is especially helpful in conflict situations. Emotional intelligence refers to the ability to be aware of your emotions (both positive and negative) and being able to channel them in a positive direction. Being empathetic relates to your ability to understand what others are thinking and feeling.

Understanding your feelings and what the are other person is feeling is very helpful in having a productive discussion.

When conflicts occur, there are two questions to ask.

1. **Where do we disagree?** I have heard people say, *"We disagree on everything."* That's often not the case. People usually disagree on one or more of the following: goals, plans, priorities, responsibilities, or values. It's important to clarify where you disagree. For example, *"We agree on the goals, but disagree on the plan to get there."*

2. **How important is the issue?** Is it a high, medium, or low priority? Some conflicts should be avoided simply because they are not that important.

Some of the generally accepted rules of engagement in any conflict include:

- ✓ Focus on the current issue. Don't bring up past problems.
- ✓ Seek to understand the other person's point of view.
- ✓ Stay open and be flexible.
- ✓ Yelling and name-calling are not allowed.
- ✓ Be specific and don't generalize.
- ✓ Focus on finding solutions.
- ✓ Know when a "cooling-off period" is needed.

Approaches to Dealing with Conflict

- **Directing Style**—If you have the authority position, (parent-child) you can tell the other person what the resolution is. *You're not going to the football game on Saturday. Case closed.*

    However, mandating a solution usually doesn't work out so well. The other person feels slighted and annoyed. They may comply with the decision, but plot on how to get even in the future.

    Assume you are dealing with two people in your group who are having regular conflicts, and you are using a directing style. Tell them the resolution of the current conflict. *Joe, you need to do ABC. Sue, you need to do XYZ.*

    Define what is acceptable and unacceptable behavior. State the rules of engagement they need to follow when conflicts occur. Explain the consequences that will be administered if rules are violated in the future.

- **Discussing Style**—You ask questions to fully understand the other person's position and the reasons behind their position.

Collaboration may lead to identifying other options that could satisfy both parties. *Let's go to the Italian restaurant for dinner, but let's get dessert at Busy B's Ice Cream Shop.*

The discussion may lead to a compromise. *This time we'll go to the Italian restaurant, but next time you get to pick the restaurant.*

If you are dealing with two people on your team who are having a conflict, you can facilitate a discussion. Ask each person for their views on the issue. Then ask each person for their view of a fair resolution. If an agreement between the two people can't be reached, revert to a directing style and tell them the resolution you expect them follow.

- **Delegating Style**—When I was young and having a conflict (or fight) with one of my brothers, my father would say, *You two need to go off and come up with a solution that you both can live with. If you can't, you're both going to be punished.* That motivated us. My brother and I discussed the issue and always arrived at a solution.

Another example of delegation—if two people in your group are having conflicts, you could delegate the task of having them work together to resolve the conflict and establish 3-to-5 rules they agree to follow in future conflict situations.

Summary—Conflicts

As a parent, teacher, coach, manager, and team leader, consider the following:

1. *Directing Style*—Define the rules of engagement.
2. *Discussing Style*—Ask questions to determine where you agree and disagree. Discuss options that would be acceptable to both parties. Acknowledge people for being open and willing to compromise.
3. *Delegating Style*—After an initial discussion, have each person go off on their own and come up with 1-to-3 possible solutions. Meet later to discuss and select the best option.

Sometimes the only solution is "agree to disagree."

Comments from Practitioners
David Hurst, Minister

"As a minister, part of my job involves helping people who are having problems or conflicts. The issues run the gamut from alcohol, drugs, marital issues, financial and interpersonal. Their problem is usually impacting several other people.

I start by meeting with the person one-on-one in a private setting. We always start with a prayer. That helps people relax and talk more truthfully about what's happening.

Discussing Style—I start by asking questions to unpack the problem. Probing questions are focused on identifying the reasons behind the behavior. Once the problem is clarified, I ask questions about what have they tried and what were the results.

Directing Style—In some situations, I suggest or tell them what to do. *You need to go to AA meetings starting tonight.*

Delegating Style—In some cases, I have made arrangements for the person to speak with someone in the congregation who has dealt with a similar problem. I would schedule the meeting and make the introductions.

In all cases, follow up is important. You have to make sure people do what they committed to do."

Chapter 9
Holding People Accountable

You need to hold people accountable for what they commit to do.

Holding people accountable requires you to monitor people's performance and take appropriate action as required. The sooner you address performance issues, the better.

These are difficult conversations, so preparation is key.

When addressing performance issues keep these points in mind.

- ✓ Know your goals
- ✓ Determine the style or approach you will use to run the meeting
- ✓ Have the facts and some specific examples
- ✓ Be prepared to listen to their explanations

Approaches to Holding People Accountable

- **Directing Style**—Tell him specifically where his performance missed the mark. Explain what he needs to do to correct the situation. Describe the consequences if improvement doesn't occur.

    Dan Rockwell, the founder of the blog, Leadership Freak said, "Use 'you' when establishing accountability. Don't say 'we' when you mean 'you'."

    When performance continues to be below expectations, most companies follow progressive discipline—verbal warning, written warning, final written warning, and termination. However, the discipline you administer needs to be appropriate for the type of violation that occurred.

- **Discussing Style**—Start by asking questions that require the person to comment what they did and why. How does he see the situation. Does he take responsibility or blame others?

   Once the problem is defined, move on to these types of questions.

   > *What changes are needed going forward?*
   > *Are you committed to making those changes?*
   > *What should the consequences be if the behavior is repeated in the future?*
   > *What did you learn from this experience?*

- **Delegating Style**—Instruct the person to go off on his own and think about his performance. Ask them to identify where he missed the mark and what should happen next.

   Set a time to meet to discuss his reflections. *Let's meet tomorrow at 9:00 am. I'm eager to hear what you come up with.*

   The person needs to be responsible and hold himself accountable for both what he did and what he needs to do going forward.

Holding people accountable requires follow-up to make sure the required changes are happening. When you see the desired changes being made, praise the person and reinforce the new behavior.

Summary—Holding People Accountable

As a parent, teacher, coach, manager, and team leader, consider the following:

1. *Directing Style*—Tell the person their performance isn't meeting your expectations. Define the required changes that they should make.
2. *Discussing Style*—Ask questions to allow the person to explain their performance.
3. *Delegating Style*—Empower the person to examine their own behavior and come up with solutions. Then, review them with you.

Some accountability issues are due to unclear expectations, lack of required resources, and work overload. Reduce confusion by making one person responsible for each task or project.

Comments from Practitioners

Leah Amico, Coach, Parent, Professional Speaker & 3-Time Olympic Gold Medalist

"When it comes to relationships and team chemistry issues, I use a style that is appropriate based on the personality of the athlete. Therefore, I believe it is crucial to get to know each person on a personal level. My philosophy is, 'coach the person before the athlete.'

Holding people accountable is very important. When problems occur, I use a **discussing** style with athletes who take responsibility for their actions. Dealing with athletes who tend to make excuses or point fingers, I use a **directing style.**

As a parent there are times when you must deal with a child who is experiencing strong emotions such as anger, frustration, fear, sadness, and anxiety. I usually start by trying to have a **discussion,** but that does not always work when emotions are running high. I have found that using a **delegating style** allowed my children some time to step back and reflect on what they were thinking and feeling. It gave them a chance to calm down and define their problem and identify some possible actions to take.

Holding people accountable to the standards and expectations you establish helps them achieve their goals and become their best self. It also establishes a positive environment for living, working, and competing."

David Hurst, Minister

"Most churches have outreach programs to prisons, hospitals, homeless shelters etc. Other church programs include Spiritual Discussion groups and Bible Study groups. In all of these initiatives, someone, usually a Deacon, volunteers to take the lead role in making it happen.

Part of my job is holding people accountable or making sure people do what they committed to do.

Directing Style—At our monthly meetings, I have the responsible person report on their task or project. They provide an update to the full group.

Discussing Style—If the person isn't doing what they signed up to do, I conduct a meeting to find out why. These are "volunteer positions," so I have to be supportive and persuasive to get them on track.

Delegating Style—On occasion, I have asked Deacons to recommend a new approach or changes to the project he is leading."

Chapter 10
Provide the Right Amount

To grow healthy plants, you need to provide the right amount of water, sunlight, fertilizer, and pruning. Too much or too little water will hurt your plants; too much or too little sunlight may cause your plants to die. The best gardeners learn what each plant needs to grow and blossom.

In a similar way, the best leaders provide the right amount of direction, discussion, and delegation to achieve the best results. Either too much or too little can have an adverse impact.

•Direction, Discussion, Delegation

Directing Style

How much information is needed?

Do not overwhelm people with data dumps. Information overload is common these days. When leaders provide too much direction, people get overwhelmed and confused. Not good!

On the other hand, don't under-communicate or omit important details. When people don't get the information they need, they underperform.

How direct and candid do you need to be?

Some people lack the courage to be frank and direct when it comes to discussing difficult topics. They skirt around the issue and sugarcoat the message. Not useful.

On the other hand, some people are too direct and uncaring. *"Ray, I did not ask your opinion. Just do it and get the hell out of my office!"* Being direct does not imply being condescending or demeaning. Direct means you say what is on your mind in a clear, respectful, and professional manner.

Two questions to ask yourself:

1. How direct do I need to be with this person in this situation?
2. What information and details do I need to provide so the person knows what to do and how to do it.

Discussing Style

"Too much discussion" can be as bad as "too little discussion." Some people let the discussion go on and on. They never get closure. They waste time.

At the other extreme, some leaders cut off the discussion too soon and force decisions that some people may not support.

Three questions to ask yourself:

1. What questions need to be discussed?
2. How will I make sure everyone has an opportunity to comment on the issue?

3. How should the final decision be made? (Consensus, majority rule, or I will decide)

Delegating Style

Don't over-delegate to your top performers. Assigning too much work to your star performers leads to burn-out.

At the other extreme, don't avoid giving other people a chance to show what they can do. Don't under-delegate.

Some people think they need to be directly involved in every problem and decision. They don't.

Give people a chance to show what they can accomplish. Proper delegation develops your children, students, and staff.

Two questions to ask yourself:

1. Am I delegating the right tasks and projects to each person?
2. Am I receiving the appropriate feedback to ensure proper progress is being made on each task?

Providing the right amount of direction, discussion, and delegation does not mean moderation in all things. For example, in some cases it may be best to provide no coaching. Let the person figure things out for himself. In other situations, a significant amount of direction and coaching may be required.

Results Achieved

When you provide the right amount of what's needed, you give people exactly what they need to get the task done. You also provide people with the challenges and questions that require them to grow and develop.

When you get it right, people say things like:

- "Your coaching was perfect."
- "Your direction was just what I needed."
- "Your questions helped me identify the real problem."

Comments from Practitioners

Al Kasper, President, Savage Arms

"I try to get to know everyone. Each person is unique. That helps me determine how direct or indirect to be.

To start the day, I give a high five, so to speak, to all the employees in my area. Their body language gives me an indication if there are any work or personal issues. I offer to talk privately with anyone who may want to.

You must be flexible in your approach. I have one manager who is overly direct—all the time. That inflexibility is limiting his career advancement."

Bill Condon, Vice President of Payroll, CBS

"Discussion is a healthy way of getting 'buy-in' from the group. However, sometimes I must cut off the individual who talks too much in order to avoid not losing the commitment of the entire group. I try to get the quiet people involved. My goal is to have a healthy sharing of opinions, so all team members have a vested interest in the decision we make. It's important to hear all viewpoints, but also make timely decisions. It's a judgment call as to when to close the discussion and move to a decision."

Rostow Ravanan, CEO and MD, Mindtree

"The boundary between over-delegation and under-delegation is generally discovered only on a case-to-case basis. If the person you have delegated to does not complete the task within the expected timeframe and/or with the desired quality, you know you have hit a roadblock. Until such a situation arises, it is better to delegate.

In my experience, I have found that more delegation is generally better for two reasons. The first is that it allows the team that reports to you to learn and grow as they take more responsibility. The second is that it frees up your time to take up higher-value tasks which leads to your growth."

Chapter 11
Continuous Improvement

Becoming an effective coach, parent, teacher, supervisor, manager, project leader, and team leader is a lifelong journey. It never ends.

Becoming your best requires a commitment to continuous improvement. A commitment to learning from mentors, colleagues, and self-study. It also requires reflection and a willingness to try new approaches.

Action Items

At the end of each week, assess your performance on how well you used each leadership style, as well as how you diagnosed each situation. Here are some questions to get you started.

Directing Style

- Were my directions clear and precise?
- Did I communicate information that was relevant and meaningful?
- Did I consistently set deadlines on assigned tasks?
- Were there any situations where I was too direct or not direct enough?
- Did I help people develop their skills and character traits?

Discussing Style

- Where there any situations where I engaged in too much discussion or too little discussion?
- Did I ask the right questions in each meeting?

- Did I listen and observe body language to understand what people were thinking and feeling?
- Was my listen/talk ratio appropriate?
- Did I help people develop their skills and character traits?

Delegating Style

- Were there any situations where I delegated too much or too little?
- Did I delegate the right tasks to the right people?
- Did I set deadlines on all delegated tasks?
- What can I do to be a more effective delegator?
- Did I help people develop their skills and character traits?

Diagnosing the Situation

- Did I misdiagnose any situations? What did I miss?
- Did I change my diagnosis as I gained more information?
- What do I need to do to fully understand the current environment?
- What new factors should I include when diagnosing situations?

Additional actions to help you improve.

1. Ask your mentor and colleagues for feedback on your effectiveness at using each of the leadership styles.
2. Observe the style and approaches that other people use in various situations.

Personal Development Plan

Each month, identify <u>one action</u> that you will take to improve your effectiveness at using one of the three leadership styles.

Find a colleague who is working on improving his/her leadership effectiveness and ask if they are willing to be your "accountability partner?"

Check in on a regular basis and learn from each other.

About the Author

Paul B. Thornton conducts seminars and workshops on alignment, leadership, and implementing change. He is a writer, speaker, and uses all three leadership styles every day! Although, when he delegates to his wife, it does not always work as expected.

He studied management, psychology, and political science at Ohio University. He was fortunate to take courses taught by Dr. Paul Hersey and Dr. Ken Blanchard. Their courses ignited his lifelong interest in management and leadership.

Paul continued his education and earned master's degrees in business (MBA) and education (MEd).

Key Experiences and Awards

- Directly involved in designing and delivering leadership training programs, succession planning, organizational change initiatives, and leading all aspects of the human resource function.
- In 1985 and 1996, he was the recipient of the United Technologies Award for Extraordinary Management Effectiveness.
- In 2015, he was the recipient of the Joseph J. Deliso Sr. Endowed Chair at Springfield Technical Community College.
- Paul has published over 100 articles in business and leadership magazines, journals, and websites.
- He is the author of eighteen books, including:
  - *The Leadership Process*
  - *Is Your Organization Aligned?*
  - *Leadership: Perfecting Your Approach and Style*

- *Leadership Case Studies*
- *Leadership—Off the Wall (WestBow Press)*

➢ Paul created twenty-eight management and leadership videos that can be found on YouTube (Search—Paul Thornton, STCC).

His wife, MJ (Mary Jean), is a former executive vice president at Travelers Insurance. She is also a professor emeritus of business administration at Capital Community College.

Paul and MJ have two adult children: Kate (married to Corey) and Andy (married to Jess), and five extra-special, super-talented grandsons: Anthony, Dominic, Keegan, Noah, and Owen.

Paul and MJ love to watch them play basketball, hockey, soccer, baseball, and lacrosse.

Paul can be contacted at pbthornton74@gmail.com.

Recommended Books and Articles

- *Developing Versatile Leaders* by Robert Kaplan and Rob Kaiser (article in the *MIT Sloan Management Review*)
- *Management of Organizational Behavior* by Paul Hersey and Ken Blanchard
- *Take Charge of You: How Self-Coaching Can Transform Your Life and Career Hardcover* by David Novak and Jason Goldsmith
- *The Leader's Window: Mastering the four styles of leadership to build high performing teams* by John Beck and Neil Yeager
- *The Leadership Engine* by Noel Tichy with Eli Cohen
- *The Leadership Process* by Paul B. Thornton
- *The Work of Leadership* by Ronald Heifetz and Donald Laurie (article in *Harvard Business Review*)
- *The Situational Leader* by Paul Hersey
- *You can't win at golf with one club: Effective leaders excel in five dimensions* by Ellen Samiec and Scott Cambell (article in *Leadership Excellence*)
- *Working without a net*: *How to survive and thrive in today's high risk business world* by Morris Schechtman

Paul B. Thornton

Leadership Styles

www.ingramcontent.com/pod-product-compliance
Lightning Source LLC
Chambersburg PA
CBHW050253220526
45465CB00002B/670